Quick Guide to Restoring Your Credit

Betsy Taylor

ISBN: 1-4823-0831-2
ISBN-13: 9781482308310
Library of Congress Control Number: 2013902029
CreateSpace Independent Publishing Platform
North Charleston, South Carolina

Dedication

I would like to dedicate this book to my husband because through it all, I was able to accomplish something I thought was never possible, rebuilding my credit.

Acknowledgments

I would like to take this opportunity to acknowledge my husband and daughter. Thank you for always being there for me and encouraging me to write this book to help others. I Love You Both!

Chapter 1
HOW DID I GET HERE

Having good credit plays an important role in what you can establish in life. Without good credit it is very difficult to own your own home, get a credit card, open a bank account and believe it or not getting a job is included in this list. In college, I had obtained several credit cards. I found out the hard way how important your credit is to you. Being a young adult with not a lot of responsibility, I found myself opening quite a few retail accounts and not managing my money well nor saving any for a rainy day. I was only concerned about buying the latest clothes and shoes in the department stores and not realizing I had to pay all of the money back for what I was purchasing with these credit cards. It is very easy to get caught up in credit card debt in college. I saw how easy it was to make purchases but I did not realize that in the end it had to be paid back with interest. Most young full time college students either do not work or only have a part time job. I didn't understand the concept of having the ability to purchase the merchandise right away and ultimately having to pay it back plus more than I paid for it because interest was being added on. My part time job was not paying full time pay. Therefore, I really couldn't afford all of the purchases I was making. It was so tempting to open up a credit card with a retailer because they would offer a percentage or an amount off of your purchase for the entire day when opening up a new account. I thought that was a great deal. I wanted to shop all day. I love to shop and it certainly came with a price.

I came to realization once I graduated from college, got married and had my daughter. It was definitely an eye opener when trying to buy a house and was denied. That was definitely a wakeup call. I knew that I had to make a difference in what I was doing. This was something I needed to do quickly.

I first thought that I could fix my credit quickly by going to a debt consultant that claimed their company could fix my credit instantly. If it seems too good to be true, most likely it is. Please don't waste your money as I did thinking this would be possible because it is not. These companies that offer these tactics tell you exactly what you want to hear and get your money and do nothing to help. I could have taken that money and paid my past due credit card bills with it. If you have considered this, please think again. I do not want you to go down the same path I traveled. This method does not work. These companies will make you promises that they cannot keep. Also, do not let anyone tell you that you should file bankruptcy. Filing for bankruptcy should not be used as a tactic to repair your credit. Bankruptcy will not improve your credit. Sometimes your credit gets worse after filing bankruptcy. Once you file Chapter 7, 11 and 13 bankruptcy it appears as a public record and could stay on your credit report up to ten years after you have filed. Chapter 13 bankruptcy public records tend to come off of your credit report sooner than the others. Chapter 13 bankruptcy may come off of your credit report in seven years. You will continue to have issues getting loans and credit cards. When applying for loans the lenders will ask you if you have ever filed bankruptcy. So even after the seven to ten years have gone by, you still have to pay the price for filing bankruptcy. You need to take the money that you would pay this debt consultant or attorney for assisting you with a bankruptcy and pay it towards any outstanding debt that you have. By paying the outstanding debt, it will in fact help you in the long run.

I wanted to write this book to help others that may have gone through a similar situation as I did or is going through it now. There is light at the end of the tunnel. Trust me, with a lot of praying and managing my money right, I did it and so can you. Pay attention to the information I have provided in this book and you are sure to get your credit back on track. It will be well worth it in the end. You will see.

Chapter 2
GET A COPY OF YOUR CREDIT REPORT

Most of us know how good or bad our credit is. There may be accounts on your credit report that does not belong to you and/or needs to be disputed because the balance shown is not correct or the account was already paid off. Identity theft is on the rise. People that you least expect will use your personal information to get credit in your name. There are also people in this world that prey on innocent victims and create scams to get your information so they can impersonate you to obtain credit. Check your credit report carefully because there may be accounts that are showing on your credit report that someone else may have opened in your name. These situations will happen from time to time so requesting a copy of your credit report is the first step to getting your credit back on track. Knowing what is on your credit report will definitely help you with this process.

Start by contacting all three Credit Bureaus:

Equifax
Credit Insurance Services, Inc.
PO Box 740241
Atlanta, GA 30374

Telephone Number: 1-800-685-1111
Website: www.equifax.com
TransUnion
Annual Credit Report Request
PO Box 105281
Atlanta, GA 30348-5281

Telephone Number: 1-877-322-8228
Website: www.transunion.com

Experian
PO Box 9556
Allen, TX 75013

Telephone Number: 1-888-397-3742
Website: www.experian.com

*Experian mailing address changes, so please call their toll free number to verify prior to writing, if writing to them is the option that you choose.

You can call, write or visit the website of each of the credit bureaus to inquire about obtaining a free copy of your credit report. You can also retrieve a free credit report by visiting the following website: www.annualcreditre-port.com

You are entitled to a free credit report once per year. I encourage you to take advantage of this each year. There is some cost associated with requesting your credit report if you have already received a free report within a 12 month period. The last time I checked, the cost was between $11 - $15 if you request another copy of your credit report. Also, if you were recently denied credit, you can also obtain a free copy of your credit report under the FACT Act. The denial letter that you received will provide you with information on which credit bureau the company used to influence their decision to deny your request for credit. You have to request the free copy of your report within 60 days of receiving the letter. The denial letter will also provide you with the name, address and telephone number for the credit bureau that the company used. You should request a copy of your credit report to see what influenced the creditor to deny your request for credit.

The credit reporting agencies reports and format of the data is a little different. However, all of the credit reports contain the same type of information. Your social security number, date of birth and employer information are all pieces of information that are used to identify you. This information is updated when you provide information to lenders.

When you receive your credit report there will be various pieces of data included in the report. The report will include personal identifying information, inquiries, collections/judgments and accounts. Examine each section closely to ensure that it is accurate.

The personal identifying information will include your name, address, social security number, date of birth and employer information. Updates to this information come from the information that you supply to lenders when trying to obtain credit. This information is not used in the credit scoring process.

The collections and/or judgments include accounts that were made public record by the county and/or state courts. It could also include information from overdue accounts from collection agencies. Bankruptcies and/or foreclosures are considered public records and will show up as well.

Credit inquiries show up on your credit report when you apply for credit. You authorize the lender to request for a copy of your credit report. If you've ever wondered how an inquiry gets on your credit report, this is how. These inquiries stay on your credit report for as long as two years. There are voluntary and involuntary inquiries. Voluntary inquiries are when you request for credit. This request gives the lender the ability to obtain a copy of your credit report. This will show on your credit report as a voluntary inquiry. Are you aware that when you get a new mobile phone, rent a rental car, request for a credit line increase and/or open a new satellite account, that these are also considered inquiries that will be added to your credit report? You want to be careful when opening up new accounts because you do not want these inquiries to negatively affect your credit score. Involuntary inquiries are when lenders send you the pre-approved credit offers through the mail. The credit bureaus provide information to the credit card companies and lenders so they may offer pre-approved offers to consumers. You can contact the credit bureaus to remove yourself from these involuntary inquiries.

If you would like to opt out of receiving pre-approved credit card mailings from credit card companies and lenders, you can visit the following website: www.optoutprescreen.com or by calling: 1-888-5-OPT OUT (1-888-567-8688) Opting out of receiving pre-approved credit card mailings will stop any future pre-screened credit card mailing offers.

The credit accounts that you have with various lenders will also show on your credit report. This includes mortgage loans, credit cards, automobile loans and etc. The credit bureau will report the type of account, the date the account was opened, your credit limit or the original loan amount, the account balance and the payment history for each account.

Once you receive your credit report, examine it for any discrepancies. If you find an account listed that is not accurate, file a dispute. You can file a dispute by phone, mail or on the credit bureau's website. The contact information for the various credit bureaus is listed at the beginning of this chapter. There should also be information at the beginning of your credit report that provides you with steps on how to notify the credit bureaus if there is a discrepancy with the information that was provided.

The credit bureau and the company that reports your information to the credit bureau is responsible for correcting any information that is not accurate or complete. You can contact the credit bureau and provide them with the information that you believe is inaccurate. When providing a copy of your credit report, be sure to highlight and/or circle the information so there is no question as to what you are disputing. If you have the documents showing why you think it is incorrect, be sure to make copies and provide it to the credit bureau. Also include detail in regards to why you think the information on your credit report is not accurate and request that the information be corrected or removed. If the credit bureau cannot verify that the information on your credit report is accurate, they must remove the information from your credit report. Keep the original copies of the information that is mailed to the credit bureau and send your copies of information with a delivery confirmation so you have proof that the credit bureaus received.

The credit bureaus have 30 days to research the discrepancies that you have informed them of. The credit bureaus will then contact the company that reported the inaccurate information to them and let them know of your dispute. The company then investigates the dispute and reports their findings back to the credit bureau. If the company finds that the information was inaccurate, they have to notify all three credit bureaus of the update to your information on your credit report. The credit bureau will notify you in writing and should also provide you with a copy of your credit report showing the updated information. If the credit bureau does not provide you with an updated copy of your credit report, you should request that they provide you with one.

If the incorrect information on your credit report, hindered you from being approved by another company and/or getting a job, you can request that the credit bureau send an updated copy of your credit report to anyone that requested a copy in the past six months. If the report was requested for employment purposes within the last two years, you can request that the credit report be sent to those requestors again with the updated information.

If the information on your credit report is accurate, you can contact the creditor to inquire about working with them to get the negative information removed from your credit report. The creditor may be willing to work with you to remove any negative remarks about late payments in exchange for you bringing your account current or making a partial settlement of your debt with them. Late payments can stay on your credit report for up to seven years. You will need to make sure that you get any settlement details in writing from the company. Once the debt arrangement has been settled, you will need to request for a copy of your credit report to make sure that the negative information was removed. If your credit report was not updated, will you will need to file a dispute with the credit bureaus and provide copies of the settlement details and a copy of your payment (if applicable) so your credit report can be updated.

There are also credit monitoring companies online that will give you access to view your credit report and credit score online. Some will even provide explanations for you in regards to the steps you can take to increase your credit score. You can gain access to your credit report online by the visiting the following website: www.freecreditreport.com

The advertisement leads you to believe that it is free; however, it is free for a period of time. Once that time has passed, you will be billed a monthly fee that will be charged to the credit card you used when setting up your account initially. There is another website that is totally free. It is: www.creditkarma.com

These online credit report reviewing websites allow you to log in and view your credit report and credit score. You have the option to print the information as well. I actually like the concept of the online credit reporting reviewing websites that allow you the ability to see your credit report at any time. You can also setup alerts and customize the information that you see in the way you would like the information displayed and/or received. There is no credit card required to get access to your credit score with some of these companies. Their online tools allow you to see all of your debt on one screen in more detail by credit cards, auto and mortgage. They also have sections that show you ways to save on your credit cards each month as well as your mortgage and automobile loans.

Some of these companies offer all three credit reports and credit scores to their members. Once you log in, some of companies will provide you with information on how many days are left before you are eligible to receive your updated credit score from all three credit bureaus. You become eligible to get your free credit scores every ninety days. Also by being a member with some of these companies, you accumulate rewards dollars that allow you to spend these dollars towards purchasing gift cards and/or merchandise.

There are also alert sections that will advise you when you have reached a certain credit score that you originally set. So for an example, if you set an alert to notify you when your credit score reach 760, you would be able to see this in your alert center while logged into your account. You would also receive an email and/or text message with this information if you chose this option in your alerts setting. You can also choose to have the alert to notify you of new or suspicious activity on your credit report. With some of these companies, your credit score can be refreshed once per day and your credit score is updated twice per month. In the event you have received an alert and would like to view your current credit score, you can do so by refreshing the credit score by clicking the refresh button next to the credit score.

Accessing your credit report information through a credit reporting viewing website may be beneficial to you. I suggest that you research the company to see how it may help you with getting your credit back on track. I found these companies to be very helpful. Compare the companies that you may be interested in and go with the company that works best for you.

Have you ever wondered how your credit score is calculated? It is calculated from different pieces of data that is in your credit report. Your credit score considers both positive and negative information that is in your credit report.

The data is grouped into five categories which are:

Payment History – 35%
Amounts Owed – 30%
Length of Credit History – 15%
New Credit – 10%
Type of Credit Used – 10%

I have provided more details for you below about the 5 categories:

Payment History – 35%

The lender wants to know if you've paid past credit accounts on time. This is the most important factor in your credit score. If you had late or missed payments, it considers how late the payments were, how much was owed, how recently they occurred, and how many there are. Late payments can stay on your credit report for up to seven years. A good track record of no late payments will increase your credit score.

It is very important to make your payments on time. If you are able to pay more than the minimum payment, do so. If not, at least pay the minimum amount before or on the due date. You may want to get in the habit of only making charges to your credit cards that you can pay off the next month. This method will save you money on interest charges.

Amounts Owed – 30%

A high percentage of your available credit being used indicates you are overextended and more likely to make late or missed payments. Your total balance on your last statement is generally the amount that will show on your credit report. Your credit score also considers the amount you owe on different types of accounts, such as credit cards and installment loans. Having a low credit utilization ratio can be much better than having a high one or even none at all.

Do not max out your credit cards or your available credit on installment loans. You should not be utilizing any more than 30% - 40% of your available credit. It helps your credit report if your utilization percentage is low.

Length of Credit History – 15%

Your credit score takes into account how long your credit accounts have been established which includes the age of your oldest and newest account as well as an average age of all of your accounts, how long certain credit accounts have been opened and how long it has been since you have used specific accounts.

If you are possibly thinking of closing any of your older credit cards, it is important to take a close look at them prior to closing those accounts. The older credit cards play an important role in the percentage that is used to determine the length of your credit history.

New Credit – 10%

Your credit score is affected by how many new accounts you have by the type of the account. It may also look at how many of them are new. Your credit score also looks to see how long it has been since you opened a new account by account type. Late payment behavior in the past can be overcome. Re-establishing your credit and making your payments on time will raise your credit score over time.

You do not want to open up to many new accounts. Having several new accounts opened will negatively impact the percentage that is used to determine the new credit category.

Type of Credit Used – 10%

Your credit score will consider various retail accounts, finance company accounts, credit cards, installment loans and mortgage loans. Installment loans and credit cards with good payment history will raise your credit score.

The percentages above are based on the importance of the five categories for the general population. The importance of any one factor in your credit score calculation depends on the overall information in your credit report. One factor for you may have a larger impact than it would for someone with a different credit history. As the information in your credit report changes, so does the importance of any factor that determines your credit score.

Chapter 3
PAY ANY LATE ACCOUNTS

When trying to get back on track with your credit, it is extremely important to make sure you pay your accounts on time. Making late payments can hurt your credit. I am sure you are aware of any accounts that you have not paid. If you are not sure, the credit report will show you any accounts that you are currently showing thirty days or more past due. The second step to getting your credit back is paying any late accounts. You want to bring any late accounts that you have to current status. You do not want to start this process with any outstanding or past due accounts.

If you have a credit card payment that is due on the 15th and you cannot make the payment until the 21st, don't skip the payment because you do not have the money at the time of payment. Yes, it will be considered late by your credit card company but it is important to pay the bill and have it post to your account before the end of the month. You will have to pay a late fee charge to your credit card company but it is better to get it paid than not to pay it at all and it shows negatively on your credit report. You want to also make sure you are paying your payment by the due date or before because you want to eliminate any additional money you have to pay to the creditor for late fees. Those late fees will add up. Please try to avoid paying your payment late. If you choose to make your payments online, be sure you pay the payment by the cut-off time so it is applied to your account the day you are making the payment. I would suggest that you pay your payments days before your payment is due to minimize the risk of paying it late online.

A history of late payments can really hurt you when you try to apply for a credit card, car and/or mortgage. This alerts the creditors that you are not worthy of paying on time when the payment is due. That is why it is important for you to make current on any bills that you are currently past due on. Call the creditors up, if you need to, and explain your situation to them. Most of them will work with you on your past due debt. It never hurts to ask. If you have to, setup payment arrangements on any accounts that you are severely default on. Doing so will prevent that debt from going to the Collection Agency.

Also look at the balances you owe on any current accounts. You will need to start paying the balances down so that you are not utilizing more than 30% - 40% of your credit limit. The lower your utilization percentage is the better. You want to start displaying a low balance to limit ratio. This will have a tremendous impact on your credit score. You can start working on this by paying more than the minimum payment due. I absolutely recommend this. If your minimum payment is $50, pay $100. If you can pay more, do so. This allows you to pay off the debt in a much quicker speed than you would have by just paying the minimum payment. Most credit card companies will show you how much it would cost you to pay the minimum amount each month and the amount it would cost you if you paid more. Pay attention to this information each month. This information is very helpful. It also allows for less interest to accumulate that you would be paying on the remaining balance of your credit card. Ultimately, if you are able to, pay the balance off each month. One suggestion would be to use the credit card for gas and pay it off each month.

You have to begin to think more responsibly when charging transactions to your credit cards. Managing your credit responsibly will definitely help with improving your credit score.

Chapter 4
Apply for New Credit

Once you have gotten all of your past due accounts current and making regular monthly payments on time, it is now time for you to apply for new credit. It is important that you attempt to establish new credit so your credit report reflects that you are currently managing any new debt responsibly also. The below credit card website was a tremendous help with getting my credit back on track. However, I will say there is some cost associated with getting your credit right.

You can visit the following website to apply for credit: www.creditcards.com. You should know the type of credit that you have, so be sure to select the appropriate category on the left navigation bar. Once you choose the appropriate category, it will show you various credit cards that meet your current situation. There is a list of different companies that provide credit cards to people with less than perfect credit. There are also credit card companies listed that offer prepaid credit cards. If you are trying to rebuild your credit, you may want to stay away from the prepaid credit cards. When using a prepaid credit card, the money has to be in the account in order to use it. In my opinion, this does not show that you are managing your credit. The prepaid credit card is considered a secure credit card because you can only spend the amount that you deposit to the account. It does not help you with re-establishing your credit.

There are a few credit card companies that you can choose from. Some of the companies will provide you with detailed information on the credit card but some will direct you to their website to obtain the additional information. It is important that you visit each of their websites to find out the details on each of the credit cards that you are interested in. Once you have taken a look at the website, you can then decide which credit card will work best for you.

These companies charge an initial processing/setup fee that could range from $80–$150 and have high interest rates. They also have high annual fees that could range from $45–$99. There are also monthly maintenance fees that they add to your account each month. The monthly maintenance fee can range from $5–$8 per month. When I asked one of the representatives about the monthly maintenance fee that appears on each statement, I was told that the fee is for the credit card company reporting the account to the credit bureau.

They will most likely start your credit limit off with a small amount to see if you are able to manage your account. Most credit card rebuilding companies will provide you with a credit limit somewhere in the range of $300–$500. You have to remember, they want to make sure you will be worthy of repaying this debt. After you have been with them for at least 6 months to a year, you could possibly request for a credit limit increase. Keep in mind that when requesting this, it will come with a price. They will charge you anywhere from $25–$50 for a $100 credit line increase. This fee will also be taken from your available balance.

When you receive your credit card, all of the charges such as the introductory/setup fee, monthly maintenance fee and annual credit card fee, will be deducted from your available credit balance. The available balance will be much less than anticipated. So for an example:

Your credit card limit is $300

Introductory/Setup fee $90

Monthly maintenance fee $6

Annual credit card fee $99

Total fees $195

When you receive your card, your available credit will be $105. Are you surprised by the amount? This may seem like a lot of fees but to me it was worth it. I was trying to get my credit back on the right track. I knew it wouldn't be easy. I knew I had to start somewhere and it wasn't going to be simple.

I was also able to get another credit card through a well known credit card company and their fees were much lower than the other credit card companies. There was no intro-ductory/processing fee or no monthly main-tenance fee. I found that the credit limit was double or triple the amount of the other com-panies. The annual credit card fee was rela-tively inexpensive, under $20 a year.

Something else I found interesting about this additional credit card company is that they have an option that may be offered to you at the initial processing of your credit ap-plication. They could potentially start you off with a $300 credit limit and once you have paid your monthly payment on time as well as not go over your credit limit for a specific time period, they would grant an increase in your credit limit. Sometimes the amount would be triple or quadruple the original credit limit.

Chapter 5
Pay Your Bills On Time

Now that you have re-established your credit, it is important that you maintain it. You need to make sure that you continue to pay your bills on time. You now have new credit along with any existing credit you had before. You want to make sure you pay these new bills as well as any old debt on time. What really helped me with this was getting a calendar. Whether it be a pocket planner or portfolio type calendar, either one that you choose will serve its purpose. You could also print a calendar from Microsoft Word and utilize it for this task. Choose whichever calendar works best for you. Each month as the bills would come in; I would record the amount due on the calendar based on the due date. I would put an "X" on the calendar on the dates that I would receive my paycheck.

This would help me to identify three things:
1.   When I got paid
2.   When the bills were due

3. When I would need to mail the bills that had to be mailed through the postal service. Most people today are paying their bills online. That is fine; just make sure you are paying it online prior to the due date and/or before the cut-off time for paying online on the actual due date.

If paying online is the option that you choose vs. mailing your bills through the postal service, be sure you are paying it before the online payment cut-off time. You want to be sure that it is applied to your account the day that you paid. Try not to wait until the bill due date to pay it online. If possible, try to pay the bill a few days before the due date so you are sure it will be applied to your account by the due date. This will also help you with interest that is calculated on your account. The earlier that you pay the bill, less interest will be accumulated for that account. Most credit card companies, or any creditor that you are paying online, have cut-off times throughout the day and if a payment is not received by that time, it is considered received the next day. Make sure you are aware of their cut-off times. This information should be on the company's website or on the back of your billing statement under the section for online payments.

When setting up your payment calendar, you will be able to identify when your bills are due and when you receive your paycheck. This will definitely help you to manage your money more effectively as well as make sure you pay your bills on time. Record all of your bills on the calendar, whether it is your insurance premiums, utility bill, cell phone bill, credit card bill, car payment, mortgage payment or gym membership. This will be very helpful, trust me. I don't remember things as easily as I use to. If I don't have it written down, I am more likely to forget it. This method is sure to help you to not forget. Once you have mailed the bill or paid online, put a check mark beside it on your calendar so you know it has been paid.

I allow the calendar to be my guide as to what I have to pay and when. It is much simplifier this way than having to keep a mental note to remember to pay a bill. If it is a bill you can pay online, I would encourage you to do so. This not only saves a little time but it will also save you money from having to put a stamp on the envelope to mail and the cost of the check. If you have a printer, print out your online confirmation. If you do not have a printer, write down your confirmation number on your calendar and/or your monthly billing statement. You could also save a screenshot of the confirmation page and save it on your computer. That way if there is some issue with the company and your payment, you have your confirmation number to provide to them. You can also include your email address in your profile of your online account that you are paying, and most companies will email you a copy of your payment confirmation and any other alerts you sign up for. Be sure to look in your account settings for each of your online accounts and add your email address. This way you will receive any type of notifications regarding your account. You should also enable your account alert settings to receive payment confirmation and any other additional alerts for your accounts that you may be interested in.

If you have a mobile device such as a smartphone or tablet, there are also applications that will allow you to setup your payment dates for your bills. The application will allow you to enter information about the company you need to pay, the date it is due, the amount due and account number. The application also allows you to set up an alert to notify you that you have an upcoming bill that is due. You can specify the amount of days you would like for the application to notify you that the bill due date is approaching. You could utilize this application to be a reminder for you when your payments are due. Be sure to allow push notifications from the application so you are notified of any bills that are approaching the due date. You will receive a message on the screen of your mobile device that will include the name of the bill and when it is due. If you are totally electronic and do not like the pen and paper method, this is a good alternative. There are several good applications that are free. There are also some applications that charge a minimal fee. Choose the application that works best for you and how you will manage paying your bills.

If you notice at anytime that you are able to pay more than the minimum payment, please do so. This will eliminate you having to pay more interest. It also allows you to pay off the credit card balance sooner. It will ultimately help your credit score.

Also another note I would add is that when paying bills online, have a separate banking account that is used strictly for online bill paying and/or purchases. This way there is only a specific amount available in that account. I like this for added security because sometimes the 'world wide web' can be a vicious place. Do the following to minimize identity theft.

1. Don't leave your personal information lying around. I hate to say this but identity thieves could be your friends or relatives. Keeping your social security information, billing statements, checkbooks and anything else with your personal information out of sight

and in a secure location. You would be surprised that the people you trust would really steal your personal information, but it is best to be safe than sorry. Please put all of your personal items away when friends or family come over to visit.

2. Do not include your Social Security Number, Telephone Number or Driver's License on your checks. If using a check to make a purchase, this will force the clerk to look at your driver's license to verify your identity. This should help with someone stealing your identity and trying to impersonate you.

3. If you know you will be out of town for vacation and/or work and no one will be home to check the mail, put a vacation stop on your mail. You can contact your local post office and request this service. The Post Office will hold your mail from the start date you provide them. You also have the option to have the post office to deliver all of your mail that was being held on the date you specify when you return or you can pick it up from your local post office once you have return. This service can be requested at the post office and for most addresses, it can

be done online. You can check the availability of this service online once you go to the United States Postal Service website.

4. Be sure to shred any billing statements as well as any pre-qualification credit card offers. If keeping your statements for a period of time is something that you want to do, be sure to keep them in the locked file cabinet also. Most credit card companies will store your statements online for you so you do not have to keep a paper copy at home. You can log into your account at any time to access the statements. You may want to verify with your credit card company how long they store your statements online so you are aware. You can stop the pre-qualification credit card offers by calling 1-888-567-8688 to get off of their pre-screen mailing list. You will be required to provide your Social Security Number.

5. If you receive solicited telephone calls at home or on your mobile telephone, do not give any of your personal information to anyone over the phone. You can be added to the "Do Not Call" registry. This should eliminate the unwanted telemarket-

ing calls. To get on the "Do Not Call" registry, call 1-888-382-1222 from the telephone number you wish to add to the registry. It may take up to 31 days for the telemarketing calls to cease. If they do not cease from calling after 31 days from you being added to the registry, you can file a claim on the National Do Not Call Registry website. The website is: www.donotcall.gov. You can also register your telephone number on the website as well, if this is your preference. This level of caution also goes for emails that you may receive. Never click on a link in an email from an unfamiliar person. If the email asks for any of your personal information, never reply back to the sender with the requested information. Your credit card company will never request your personal information via email. Contact your credit card company if you receive a call and/or email from someone pretending to be a representative from their company. You will also be helping someone else to not get scammed by these phony tactics. The company can send out an email to all of their customers alerting them of this scam so no one becomes a victim.

6. Review your billing statements for accuracy. If you see a charge on your statement that is questionable, contact your creditor to inquire about the charge. Catching fraud early minimizes the damage a thief can do and usually results in less money and time spent having to resolve any problems that occur. The company may be able to provide added security to your account if you have become a victim. They may be able to add security measures when there are suspicious transactions charged to your account. The added security measure could result in them having to contact you or you contacting them prior to making large purchases to get authorization or the transaction could be declined.

7. Subscribe to a service that will provide you with a copy of your credit reports and score. You will get an instant notification if there are changes to your credit report or score by the credit monitoring agency. You will know quickly if someone has applied for credit in your name. This would allow you to take action quickly.

8. Install a firewall or virus-protection software on your computer. This added security will prevent a hacker or any tracking software from getting any of your private information such as banking account numbers, credit card numbers, passwords and/or social security number.

If you do detect identity theft:

1. Call the credit bureaus and get their help. In 24 hours or less, a fraud alert will be put on all your credit reports, alerting creditors to call for permission before opening any accounts in your name. Creditors aren't required by law to pay attention to fraud alerts, so you'll have to check your credit reports frequently to make sure no new accounts are opened. You can also put a security freeze on your credit report with each of the credit bureaus. The security freeze will prevent any new loans or services to be granted in your name. A security freeze may delay the approval process of credit cards or loans that you attempt to open. You will have to put a security freeze on each of your credit reports with the three different

credit bureaus. There is no fee for this if you are a victim of identity theft. If you have not experienced identity theft and would like this added security feature, visit the website for the credit bureaus to view the cost for this added protection.

Visit the following website for Equifax to put a security freeze on your credit report: www.freeze.equifax.com or call: 1-800-685-1111 or NY residents call: 1-800-349-9960

Visit the following website for Experian to put a security freeze on your credit report: www.experian.com/freeze or call: 1-888-EX-PERIAN (1-888-397-3742)

Visit the following website for TransUnion to put a security freeze on your credit report: https://annualcreditreport.transunion.com/fa/securityFreeze/landing or call: 1-888-909-8872

If you need to take the security freeze off of your credit report, you will need to contact all three credit bureaus. You can permanently remove the security freeze or you can ask the credit bureau to temporarily remove the security freeze for a period of time. Removing the security freeze permanently or temporarily will allow you to apply for credit or allow another party to access your credit report to view any transactions.

2. Change all account access infor-mation to lock thieves out of your accounts. Contact your bank and request new account numbers for all of your accounts. You will also need to request a new PIN num-ber. Close all credit card accounts and re-open them with new ac-count numbers. You may also want to contact the Social Security Ad-ministration to get a new Social Se-curity Number as well as contact the DMV for a new driver's license number. You may also want to con-tact your utility companies to inform them that someone may try to open up utility accounts in your name. You'll need to contact the local Post Office if you suspect mail theft also.

3. Contact the local police department to file a report. Provide the police de-partment with a listing of the fraudu-lent accounts. Be sure to get a copy of the report so you can provide a copy to the credit reporting agencies and creditors as proof of the crime.

4.   Keep detailed records of everything you have done to resolve the problems. This way you will have a detailed record of everything that happened and how you handled along with who you spoke with.

Chapter 6
Don't Go Over Your Limit

It is important that you use your credit cards wisely. Make sure that you do not go over your credit limit. Going over your credit limit shows the credit bureaus that you are living above your means. You should not have more than 30 – 40% of your credit limit tied up with purchases. Remember, you have to prove to the credit bureaus that you are responsible and that you have the ability to manage your credit well this time around. Show the credit bureaus that you are determined, committed and responsible. This type of behavior will grant you an increase in your credit limit. It will also boost your credit score.

By not having your credit cards maxed out will help you when trying to apply for new credit also because it shows the credit bureau and lender that you are not over extending yourself with your buying power. These are the types of characteristics that the credit bureaus and lenders look for. The creditors are more likely to provide credit to anyone whose credit report shows low risk.

Also, by going over your limit, some credit card companies will not only charge you an over the limit fee but they could possibly raise your annual percentage rate too. Be sure to monitor your spending. Charging more than your limit also hurts your credit score because it is a strong indicator of poor credit management and the creditors will look at it as high lending risk.

Do not opt in for the over the limit feature that your credit card company may offer. Don't opt in for the option of the credit card company paying if you are charging a transaction more than your available credit. Your credit card company cannot charge an over the limit fee unless you opt in. If you don't tell your credit card company that you want over the limit transactions to be processed, then those transactions will be declined and you will not be charged an over the limit fee and/or risk your annual percentage rate increasing. Some of the credit card companies will penalize you for going over your credit limit. You may want to read the fine print. Some credit card companies will charge you an over the limit fee as well as increase your annual percentage rate for going over your credit limit. They will sometimes increase your annual percentage rate for being late on a monthly payment also.

Enroll in balance alerts with your credit card company, if they have this option. You should be able to set this up in your credit card account settings. Once you setup this option you will be getting an alert, whether it is by email and/or text message when you are close to the account balance that you have specified to receive an alert on. This is a helpful feature that will allow you to stay within the 30% - 40% of your available credit of your credit card. You can calculate the 30% - 40% of your available credit to determine what amount you should set your alert for.

If you want to make a purchase and not sure how much is available on your card, contact your credit card company and find out your available credit. If you have a mobile device, you may have the ability to check your account for your available credit via the internet. Most credit card companies even have mobile applications available that will allow you to see your available credit, transactions, payments, etc, right from the mobile application. Don't risk going over your credit limit, check before you make a purchase.

Chapter 7
Learn to Save and Start a Budget

Now that you have completed all of the steps to getting your credit back on track, you need to start to save a little. It is important that you have a savings set aside for any unexpected events. Having a little money set aside will help you out with an unexpected situation that may occur. No one wants to have an unplanned event or emergency to come up and you don't have any money to help with the situation. We know that unplanned situations will come up, that's life. It is very difficult to plan for emergencies, but when you begin to save that makes the situation a little more bearable.

I would suggest creating a budget. You will need to list out all of your bills and calculate the amount of money that you bring home each month. There are expenses that you know will be the same amount each month such as your mortgage or rent, car payment, cable service, credit card payments, and insurance. There are other expenses that can vary each month such as groceries, clothing, gas, and entertainment. Do not forget to include spending money. Sometimes spending money is overlooked and not included in the budget. You want to make sure this is included so you are getting a true representation of your budget. You may be surprised to discover the amount of money you spend out on certain things each month.

Once you have gathered all of your expenses, total your monthly income and monthly expenses. You are off to a good start if there is a remaining amount from your monthly income after you subtract your monthly expenses. You can take the remaining amount and pay some towards reducing your debt by paying more on your credit cards and you can also take some of it and put in a savings account.

If you are capable of putting aside a certain amount of money out of your paycheck each pay period, please do so. You can accomplish this by transferring the money into your savings account or by setting up an automated transfer with your bank. Your employer may be able to allow you to setup more than one direct deposit account. The first direct deposit account would be your normal checking direct deposit account and the second account will allow you to have a portion of your wages direct deposited into your savings account. This could also be a way for you to have money deposited into a savings account. If you setup an automated transfer with your bank, this eliminates you having to remember to physically move the money to your savings. Sometimes relying on yourself to physically put money into a savings account is very hard for people to do. It may be easier to setup an automated transfer to savings with your employer and/or the bank so when you are paid, the money is automatically moved to your savings account. You will be surprised how much money has accumulated in your savings account over time just by starting out with a small amount.

If your expenses are greater than your monthly income, you will need to make some changes. You should not be paying out more than you are bringing home. You will need to evaluate what you are spending your money on. You may be able to save a little by cutting back on things that are not necessities. Have you thought about reducing your cable or satellite bill? This could definitely save you a little extra money each month. Contact your Cable or Satellite Company and find out what the cost would be for a package that has fewer channels. You may be paying for features that you are not utilizing. You can also browse your Cable or Satellite Company's website to gain knowledge on these various packages. You could also contact your Cable or Satellite Company to see what type of specials they have for current customers. If their specials are only for new customers, ask to speak to someone in their retention department or customer loyalty area. This department should be able to assist you and potentially provide you with some type of discount for you being a current loyal customer. They do not want to lose your business.

Do you have internet services? Most people do. You could contact your internet provider to inquire about different internet packages. This could save you a little more. Most people sign up for internet and keep the same speed for years. It is possible that the amount you are currently paying is the new promotion for a higher speed and/or the amount has dropped on the current internet speed that you have. Call to find out more. This could help you save a little more per month. You could also look at bundling this service with your home telephone service and save a little extra money each month.

I am sure most people have mobile telephones. Have you thought of switching to another plan that is less expensive than the one you currently have? Talk to your mobile carrier in regards to various packages they have. They will be able to look at your average usage and provide a plan that is suitable to your needs and pricing. You could also contact the customer retention department or customer loyalty area. They do not want to lose your business and should be willing to work something out with you.

Are you eating out a lot? If the answer is yes, try cooking at home for a change. It will be much healthier for you and less expensive. Not only will you have the ability to eat healthy foods, it will also save you some money. You could also save some of the food for leftovers so you can take to work for lunch the next day. This method is a win-win for you. You are now eating healthier foods and you are also saving money because it is ultimately less expensive than eating out. You could try this for breakfast and lunch and save an unbelievable amount of money each week.

If you have factored in entertainment in your budget, try eliminating this since it is not a necessity. Once you've had the opportunity to see a positive amount in your budget after putting money aside into your savings account, you can then add entertainment back into your budget.

You may have to get a part-time job to assist you with getting to the goal that you are working towards. A part-time job would give you the added funds that you need to pay down your credit cards. It would also give you the ability to put a little more of your money into a savings account.

Chapter 8
Check Your Credit Report Again

Now is the time for you to check your credit report again. It could take as little as six months to a year to see results. If you have followed these steps, I am sure your credit report looks much better and your score has increased a lot. You will now be able to get the house that you dreamed of owning as well as get a better interest rate on the new car you've been looking at. You can also get a better interest rate so you can finally refinance your current house.

You will also be able to get better interest rates on any new credit cards you decide to apply for. You can now replace those higher interest rate, high annual fee, monthly maintenance fee cards for a credit card that is more suited for you. You should have no problem getting a low interest rate, no annual fee and no maintenance credit card. Please remember, be careful when closing any accounts as well. This can negatively impact your credit. I am sure you want to replace the high interest rate, monthly and annual fee credit cards but do it wisely. Give new credit cards time to positively reflect on your credit report prior to closing any that you no longer want to keep because of high interest rates or fees.

You now know the five categories that have influence over your credit score. Be sure to keep these in mind so you are able to maintain your good credit. Remember to pay your bills on time. While certain bills aren't reported to the credit bureaus when you pay on time, they could end up on your credit report if you fail to pay. Keep your credit card balances low. The high balance on your credit card could drop your credit score. Your credit card balance should be within 30%–40% of your credit limit to maintain a good credit score. As I mentioned in an earlier chapter, the creditor will typically report the balance that was shown on your last billing statement and if it is a high balance, your credit score will be affected. Do not close old credit card accounts too soon. When you close a credit card account, your creditor will no longer send updates to the credit bureau and this will impact the credit scoring because it places less weight on inactive accounts. Losing that credit history will shorten your average credit age and cause your credit score to drop. Also limit any new applications for credit. Each time you apply for new credit it will affect your credit score. To maintain a good credit score now and in the future, you should open new credit sparingly. However, if you are deciding to purchase a new house or new car, please have your credit checked in the same time frame if you are considering various lenders. You do not want to let one lender pull your credit one month and then the next month let another lender pull your credit. Allow your credit to be checked with multiple lenders during the same time so it does not negatively impact your credit score. Keep a regular watch on your credit report. Now that you have your credit back on the right track, you want it to stay that way. Identity theft, credit card fraud and errors could lead to inaccurate information on your credit report. Checking your credit report throughout the year allows you to detect these mistakes sooner so you can get them corrected and maintain your good credit score.

I hope this information will help you as much as it helped me. If you follow these steps, you will be on your way to rebuilding your credit. Be patient because it does not happen overnight, but when your credit does take a turn for the better, you will be glad that you hung in there and gave your credit the attention that it needed. You will be so glad that you did.